# Celebrate Rec[illegible]

# Taking an Honest and Spiritual Inventory

## *The Journey Begins*

PARTICIPANT'S GUIDE 2

**John Baker** is the founder of Celebrate Recovery®, a ministry started at Saddleback Church. It is estimated that over the last 25 years more than 1.5 million people have gone through this Christ-centered recovery program. There are currently over 27,000 churches that have weekly Celebrate Recovery meetings.

John has been on staff since Celebrate Recovery started. He has served as the Pastor of Membership, the Pastor of Ministries, and is currently the Pastor of Saddleback Church's Signature Ministries. He is also serving as one of the nine Elder Pastors at Saddleback. John is a nationally known speaker and trainer in helping churches start Celebrate Recovery ministries.

John's writing accomplishments include Celebrate Recovery's *The Journey Begins* Curriculum, *Life's Healing Choices*, the *Celebrate Recovery Study Bible* (general editor), and *The Landing* and *Celebration Place* (coauthor). John's newest books are *Your First Step to Celebrate Recovery* and *The Celebrate Recovery Devotional* (coauthor).

John and his wife Cheryl, the cofounder of Celebrate Recovery, have been married for more than four decades and have served together in Celebrate Recovery since the beginning. They have two adult children, Laura and Johnny, and five grandchildren.

---

**Johnny Baker** has been on staff at Celebrate Recovery since 2004 and has been the Pastor of Celebrate Recovery at Saddleback Church since 2012. As an adult child of an alcoholic who chose to become an alcoholic himself, Johnny is passionate about breaking the cycle of dysfunction in his family and helping other families find the tools that will lead to healing and openness. He knows that because of Jesus Christ, and by continuing to stay active in Celebrate Recovery, Maggie, Chloe, and Jimmy—his three children—will never see him drink. Johnny is a nationally recognized speaker, trainer, and teacher of Celebrate Recovery. He is a coauthor of the *Celebrate Recovery Daily Devotional*, *Celebration Place*, and *The Landing*, and is an associate editor of the *Celebrate Recovery Study Bible*. He has been married since 2000 to his wife Jeni, who serves alongside him in Celebrate Recovery.

REVISED EDITION

# Celebrate Recovery®

# Taking an Honest and Spiritual Inventory

PARTICIPANT'S GUIDE 2

## *The Journey Begins*

A recovery program based on
eight principles from the Beatitudes

JOHN BAKER

FOREWORD BY RICK WARREN

ZONDERVAN®

ZONDERVAN

*Taking an Honest and Spiritual Inventory*


Requests for information should be addressed to:
Zondervan, *3900 Sparks Drive SE, Grand Rapids, Michigan 49546*

ISBN 978-0-310-13140-3 (softcover)
ISBN 978-0-310-13141-0 (ebook)



*Interior design: Michelle Espinoza*

*Printed in the United States of America*

# Contents

# Foreword by Rick Warren

You've undoubtedly heard the expression "Time heals all wounds." Unfortunately, it isn't true. As a pastor I frequently talk with people who are still carrying hurts from thirty or forty years ago. The truth is, time often makes things worse. Wounds that are left untended fester and spread infection throughout your entire body. Time only extends the pain if the problem isn't dealt with.

Celebrate Recovery® is a biblical and balanced program that can help you overcome your hurts, habits, and hang-ups. Based on the actual words of Jesus rather than psychological theory, this recovery program is more effective in helping people change than anything else I've seen or heard of. Over the years I've witnessed how the Holy Spirit has used this program to transform literally thousands of lives at Saddleback Church and help people grow toward full Christlike maturity.

Perhaps you are familiar with the classic 12-Step program of AA and other groups. While undoubtedly many lives have been helped through the 12 Steps, I've always been uncomfortable with that program's vagueness about the nature of God, the saving power of Jesus Christ, and the ministry of the Holy Spirit. So I began an intense study of the Scriptures to discover what God had to say about "recovery." To my amazement, I found the principles of recovery — in their logical order — given by Christ in His most famous message, the Sermon on the Mount.

My study resulted in a ten-week series of messages called "The Road to Recovery." During that series my associate pastor John Baker developed the four participant's guides, which became the heart of our Celebrate Recovery program.

As you work through these participant's guides, I trust that you will come to realize many benefits from this program. Most of all, however, my prayer for you is that, through Celebrate Recovery, you will find deep peace and lasting freedom in Jesus Christ as you walk your own road to recovery.

Dr. Rick Warren
Senior Pastor, Saddleback Church

# Introduction

The purpose of Celebrate Recovery® is to allow us to become free from life's hurts, hang-ups, and habits. By working through the eight principles of recovery based on the Beatitudes, with Jesus Christ as our Higher Power, we can and will change! We will begin to experience the true peace and serenity that we have been seeking. We will no longer need to rely on our dysfunctional, compulsive, and addictive behaviors as a temporary "fix" for our pain.

By applying the biblical principles of conviction, conversion, surrender, confession, restitution, prayer, quiet time, witnessing, and helping one another found within the eight principles, we will restore or develop stronger relationships with others and God.

You have completed the first three principles to the best of your ability: you have "gotten right with God." Now as you prepare to work Principle 4, you begin the journey of "getting right with yourself" (Principles 4 – 5).

After each lesson, there is an exercise for you to complete. Answer each question to the best of your ability. Don't worry about what you think the answer *should* be. Pray and then write down the answer from your heart. Remember John 8:32: "Then you will know the truth, and the truth will set you free."

**An important word of caution:** Do not begin this principle without a sponsor or a strong accountability partner (these are explained in Lesson 7)! You need someone you trust to help keep you balanced during this step, not to do the work for you. Nobody can do that except you. But you need encouragement from someone who will support your progress and keep you accountable. That's what this program is all about.

After you have completed the exercise, share it with someone that you trust. Your group, an accountability partner, your sponsor or a close friend in recovery are all safe choices. You do not recover from your hurts, hang-ups, and habits from just attending recovery meetings. You must work and live the principles!

In His steps,
John Baker

# The Road to Recovery

## Eight Principles Based on the Beatitudes

By Pastor Rick Warren

1. **R**ealize I'm not God. I admit that I am powerless to control my tendency to do the wrong thing and that my life is unmanageable.

   *"Happy are those who know they are spiritually poor."*
   *(Matthew 5:3)*

2. **E**arnestly believe that God exists, that I matter to Him, and that He has the power to help me recover.

   *"Happy are those who mourn, for they shall be comforted."*
   *(Matthew 5:4)*

3. **C**onsciously choose to commit all my life and will to Christ's care and control.

   *"Happy are the meek." (Matthew 5:5)*

4. **O**penly examine and confess my faults to myself, to God, and to someone I trust.

   *"Happy are the pure in heart." (Matthew 5:8)*

5. **V**oluntarily submit to every change God wants to make in my life and humbly ask Him to remove my character defects.

   *"Happy are those whose greatest desire is to do what God requires."*
   *(Matthew 5:6)*

6. **E**valuate all my relationships. Offer forgiveness to those who have hurt me and make amends for harm I've done to others, except when to do so would harm them or others.

   *"Happy are the merciful." (Matthew 5:7)*
   *"Happy are the peacemakers." (Matthew 5:9)*

7. **R**eserve a daily time with God for self-examination, Bible reading, and prayer in order to know God and His will for my life and to gain the power to follow His will.

8. **Y**ield myself to God to be used to bring this Good News to others, both by my example and by my words.

   *"Happy are those who are persecuted because they*
   *do what God requires." (Matthew 5:10)*

# Twelve Steps and Their Biblical Comparisons*

1. We admitted we were powerless over our addictions and compulsive behaviors, that our lives had become unmanageable.

   *"For I know that good itself does not dwell in me, that is, in my sinful nature. For I have the desire to do what is good, but I cannot carry it out." (Romans 7:18)*

2. We came to believe that a power greater than ourselves could restore us to sanity.

   *"For it is God who works in you to will and to act in order to fulfill his good purpose." (Philippians 2:13)*

3. We made a decision to turn our lives and our wills over to the care of God.

   *"Therefore, I urge you, brothers and sisters, in view of God's mercy, to offer your bodies as a living sacrifice, holy and pleasing to God — this is your true and proper worship." (Romans 12:1)*

4. We made a searching and fearless moral inventory of ourselves.

   *"Let us examine our ways and test them, and let us return to the Lord." (Lamentations 3:40)*

5. We admitted to God, to ourselves, and to another human being the exact nature of our wrongs.

   *"Therefore confess your sins to each other and pray for each other so that you may be healed." (James 5:16)*

6. We were entirely ready to have God remove all these defects of character.

   *"Humble yourselves before the Lord, and he will lift you up." (James 4:10)*

7. We humbly asked Him to remove all our shortcomings.

   *"If we confess our sins, he is faithful and just and will forgive us our sins and purify us from all unrighteousness." (1 John 1:9)*

8. We made a list of all persons we had harmed and became willing to make amends to them all.

   *"Do to others as you would have them do to you." (Luke 6:31)*

9. We made direct amends to such people whenever possible, except when to do so would injure them or others.

   *"Therefore, if you are offering your gift at the altar and there remember that your brother or sister has something against you, leave your gift there in front of the altar. First go and be reconciled to them; then come and offer your gift." (Matthew 5:23 – 24)*

10. We continued to take personal inventory and when we were wrong, promptly admitted it.

    *"So, if you think you are standing firm, be careful that you don't fall!" (1 Corinthians 10:12)*

11. We sought through prayer and meditation to improve our conscious contact with God, praying only for knowledge of His will for us and power to carry that out.

    *"Let the message of Christ dwell among you richly." (Colossians 3:16)*

12. Having had a spiritual experience as the result of these steps, we try to carry this message to others and to practice these principles in all our affairs.

    *"Brothers and sisters, if someone is caught in a sin, you who live by the Spirit should restore that person gently. But watch yourselves, or you also may be tempted." (Galatians 6:1)*

* Throughout this material, you will notice several references to the Christ-centered 12 Steps. Our prayer is that Celebrate Recovery will create a bridge to the millions of people who are familiar with the secular 12 Steps (I acknowledge the use of some material from the 12 Suggested Steps of Alcoholics Anonymous) and in so doing, introduce them to the one and only true Higher Power, Jesus Christ. Once they begin that relationship, asking Christ into their hearts as Lord and Savior, true healing and recovery can begin!

# Serenity Prayer

If you have attended secular recovery programs, you have seen the first four lines of the "Prayer for Serenity." The following is the complete prayer. I encourage you to pray it daily as you work through the principles!

**Prayer for Serenity**

*God, grant me the serenity*
*to accept the things I cannot change,*
*the courage to change the things I can,*
*and the wisdom to know the difference.*
*Living one day at a time,*
*enjoying one moment at a time ;*
*accepting hardship as a pathway to peace ;*
*taking, as Jesus did,*
*this sinful world as it is,*
*not as I would have it ;*
*trusting that You will make all things right*
*if I surrender to Your will ;*
*so that I may be reasonably happy in this life*
*and supremely happy with You forever in the next.*
*Amen.*

Reinhold Niebuhr

# Celebrate Recovery's Small Group Guidelines

The following five guidelines will ensure that your small group is a safe place. They need to be read at the beginning of every meeting.

1. Keep your sharing focused on your own thoughts and feelings. Limit your sharing to three to five minutes.
2. There is NO cross talk. Cross talk is when two individuals engage in conversation excluding all others. Each person is free to express his or her feelings without interruptions.
3. We are here to support one another, not "fix" another.
4. Anonymity and confidentiality are basic requirements. What is shared in the group stays in the group. The only exception is when someone threatens to injure themselves or others.
5. Offensive language has no place in a Christ-centered recovery group.

Lesson 7

# Sponsor

**Principle 4**: Openly examine and confess my faults to myself, to God, and to someone I trust.

*"Happy are the pure in heart." (Matthew 5:8)*

**Step 4**: We made a searching and fearless moral inventory of ourselves.

*"Let us examine our ways and test them, and let us return to the LORD." (Lamentations 3:40)*

## Think About It

You've heard the word "sponsor" for a few weeks now. I'm sure you have at least a vague idea of what a sponsor is, but maybe you're wondering why you even need one.

Why do I need a sponsor and/ or an accountability partner?

There are three reasons why having a sponsor is vital.

**Having a sponsor and/or accountability partner is biblical.**

*"Two are better off than one, because together they can work more effectively. If one of them falls down, the other can help him up. But if someone is alone . . . there is no one to help him. . . . Two people can resist an attack that would defeat one person alone." (Ecclesiastes 4:9 – 12, GNT)*

*"As iron sharpens iron, one person sharpens another."*
*(Proverbs 27:17)*

**Having a sponsor and/or accountability partner is a key part of your recovery program.**

Your recovery program has four key elements to success:

- To the best of your ability, maintain your **honest** view of reality as you *work* each principle. The best way to ensure this is to have a sponsor and develop a strong accountability support team.
- Make recovery group **meetings** a priority in your schedule. Knowing that a sponsor or accountability partner will be there to greet you or notice that you're not there is an added incentive to attend.
- Maintain your **spiritual program** with Jesus Christ, through prayer, meditation, and studying His Word.
- Get involved in **service**, which includes serving as a sponsor (after you have completed all eight principles) or accountability partner.

**Having a sponsor and/or an accountability partner is the best guard against relapse.**

By providing feedback to keep you on track, a sponsor and/or accountability partner can see your old dysfunctional hurts, hang-ups, and habits beginning to return, and point them out to you quickly. He or she can confront you with truth and love without placing shame or guilt.

## What are the qualities of a sponsor?

*"Though good advice lies deep within a counselor's heart, the wise man will draw it out." (Proverbs 20:5, TLB)*

When you are selecting a possible sponsor, look for the following qualities:

1. Does his walk match his talk? Is he living by the eight principles?
2. Does she have a growing relationship with Jesus Christ?
3. Does he express the desire to help others on the "road to recovery?"
4. Does she show compassion, care, and hope, but not pity?

5. Is he a good listener?
6. Is she strong enough to confront your denial or procrastination?
7. Does he offer suggestions?
8. Can she share her own current struggles with others?

## What is the role of a sponsor?

1. She can be there to discuss issues in detail that are too personal or would take too much time in a meeting.
2. He is available in times of crisis or potential relapse.
3. She serves as a sounding board by providing an objective point of view.
4. He is there to encourage you to work the principles at your own speed. He does not work the steps for you!
5. Most important, she attempts to model the lifestyle resulting from working the eight principles.
6. A sponsor can resign or can be fired.

## How do I find a sponsor and/or an accountability partner?

First, your sponsor or accountability partner MUST be of the same sex as you. After you have narrowed the field down with that requirement, listen to people share. Do you relate to or resonate with what is spoken? Ask others in your group to go out for coffee after the meeting. Get to know the person before you ask him or her to be your sponsor or accountability partner!

If you ask someone to be your sponsor or accountability partner and that person says no, do not take it as a personal rejection. Ask someone else. You can even ask for a "temporary" sponsor or accountability partner.

Ask God to lead you to the sponsor and/or accountability partner of His choosing. He already has someone in mind for you.

## What is the difference between a sponsor and an accountability partner?

A sponsor is someone who has completed the four participant's guides. He or she has worked through the eight principles and the 12 Steps. The main goal of this relationship is to choose someone to guide you through the program.

An accountability partner is someone you ask to hold you accountable for certain areas of your recovery or issues, such as meeting attendance, journaling, and so forth. This person can be at the same level of recovery as you are, unlike a sponsor, who should have completed the eight principles or 12 Steps. The main goal of this relationship is to encourage one another. You can even form an accountability team of three or four.

The accountability partner or group acts as the "team," whereas the sponsor's role is that of a "coach."

**Write About It**

1. Why is it important for you to have a support team?

2. What qualities are you looking for in a sponsor?

3. How have you attempted to find a sponsor/accountability partner?

4. What are some new places and ways you can try to find a sponsor/ accountability partner?

5. What is the difference between a sponsor and an accountability partner?

6. List the names and phone numbers of possible sponsors or accountability partners. These should be individuals you have met on your "Road to Recovery" who have touched you in the sharing of their experiences, strengths, and hopes.

Lesson 8

# Moral

**Principle 4**: Openly examine and confess my faults to myself, to God, and to someone I trust.

*"Happy are the pure in heart." (Matthew 5:8)*

**Step 4**: We made a searching and fearless moral inventory of ourselves.

*"Let us examine our ways and test them, and let us return to the LORD." (Lamentations 3:40)*

**An important word of caution:** Do not begin this principle without a sponsor or a strong accountability partner (these are explained in Lesson 7)! You need someone you trust to help keep you balanced during this step, not to do the work for you. Nobody can do that except you. But you need encouragement from someone who will support your progress and hold you accountable. That's what this program is all about.

## Think About It

In this principle, you need to list (inventory) all the significant events — good and bad — in your life. You need to be as honest as you can be to allow God to show you your part and how that affected you and others. The acrostic for MORAL shows you how to begin.

## **M**ake time

Set aside a special time to begin your inventory. Schedule an appointment with yourself. Set aside a day or a weekend to get alone with God! Clear your mind of the present hassles of daily life.

*"Then listen to me. Keep silence and I will teach you wisdom!"*
*(Job 33:33, TLB)*

## **O**pen

Open your heart and your mind to allow the feelings that the pain of the past has blocked or caused you to deny. Try to "wake up" your feelings! Ask yourself, "What do I feel guilty about? What do I resent? What do I fear? Am I trapped in self-pity, alibis, and dishonest thinking?"

*"Let me express my anguish. Let me be free to speak out*
*of the bitterness of my soul." (Job 7:11, TLB)*

## **R**ely

Rely on Jesus, your Higher Power, to give you the courage and strength this exercise requires.

*"Love the Lord, all of you who are his people; for the Lord*
*protects those who are loyal to him. . . . So cheer up! Take courage if*
*you are depending on the Lord." (Psalm 31:23 – 24, TLB)*

## **A**nalyze

Analyze your past honestly. To do a "searching and fearless moral inventory," you must step out of your denial!

That's all that the word *moral* means — honest! This step requires looking through your denial of the past into the truth!

*"The Lord gave us mind and conscience;*
*we cannot hide from ourselves." (Proverbs 20:27, GNT)*

## **L**ist

List both the good and the bad. Keep your inventory balanced! If you just look at all the bad things of your past, you will distort your inventory and open yourself to unnecessary pain.

*"Let us examine our ways and test them." (Lamentations 3:40)*

The verse doesn't say, "Examine only your bad, negative ways." You need to honestly focus on the pros *and* the cons of your past!

As you compile your inventory, you will find that you have done some harmful things to yourself and others. No one's inventory (life) is flawless. We have all "missed the mark" in some area of our lives. In recovery we are not to dwell on the past, but we need to understand it so we can begin to allow God to change us. Jesus told us, "My purpose is to give life in all its fullness" (John 10:10, TLB).

### Principle 4 Prayer

*Dear God, You know my past, all the good and the bad things that I've done. In this step, I ask that You give me the strength and the courage to list those things so that I can "come clean" and face them and the truth. Please help me reach out to others You have placed along my "road to recovery." Thank You for providing them to help me keep balanced as I do my inventory. In Christ's name I pray, Amen.*

## Write About It

1. Where will you go for quiet time to begin your inventory?

2. What date have you set aside to start? What time?

3. What are your fears as you begin your inventory? Why?

4. What can you do to help you "wake up" your feelings?

5. Describe your experience of turning your life over to Christ.

6. How do you attempt to turn over your will to God's care on a daily basis?

7. List the things you have used to block the pain of your past.

8. What have you done to step out of your denial?

9. How can you continue to find new ways out of your denial of the past?

10. Why is it important to do a written inventory?

11. What are some of the good things you have done in the past?

12. What are some of the negative things you have done in the past?

13. Do you have a sponsor or accountability partner to help you keep your inventory balanced?

Lesson 9

# INVENTORY

**Principle 4**: Openly examine and confess my faults to myself, to God, and to someone I trust.

*"Happy are the pure in heart." (Matthew 5:8)*

**Step 4**: We made a searching and fearless moral inventory of ourselves.

*"Let us examine our ways and test them, and let us return to the LORD." (Lamentations 3:40)*

## Think About It

Now that you have the background information and you've built your accountability team, it's time to start writing your inventory. This lesson will provide you with the tools you need.

### How do I start my inventory?

The Celebrate Recovery Inventory is divided into five sections. It will help you keep focused on reality and recall events that you may have repressed. Remember, you are not going through this alone. You are developing your support team to guide you, but even more important, you are growing in your relationship with Jesus Christ!

It will take you more than one page to write out your inventory. You have permission to copy the "Celebrate Recovery Principle 4 Inventory Worksheet" on pages 30 and 31.

*Column 1: "The Person"*

In this column you list the person or object you resent or fear. Go as far back as you can. Resentment is mostly unexpressed anger and fear.

*"Get rid of all bitterness, rage and anger, brawling and slander, along with every form of malice." (Ephesians 4:31)*

*Column 2: "The Cause"*

It has been said that "hurt people hurt people." In this column you are going to list the specific actions that someone did to hurt you. What did the person do to cause you resentment and/or fear? An example would be the alcoholic father who was emotionally unavailable for you as you were growing up. Another example would be the parent who attempted to control and dominate your life. This reflective look can be very painful. But . . .

*"Fear not, for I am with you. Do not be dismayed. I am your God. I will strengthen you; I will help you; I will uphold you with my victorious right hand." (Isaiah 41:10, TLB)*

*Column 3: "The Effect"*

In this column write down how that specific hurtful action affected your life. List the effects it had on your past and your present.

*Column 4: "The Damage"*

Which of your basic instincts were injured?
Social — broken relationships, slander
Security — physical safety, financial loss
Sexual — abusive relationships, damaged intimacy
No matter how you have been hurt, no matter how lost you may feel, God wants to comfort and restore you.

*"I will look for those that are lost, bring back those that wander off, bandage those that are hurt, and heal those that are sick." (Ezekiel 34:16, GNT)*

*Column 5: "My Part"*

You need to ask yourself, "What part of my resentment against another is my responsibility?" Ask God to show you your part in a broken or damaged marriage or relationship, with a distant child or parent, or maybe a lost job. In addition, list all the people whom you have hurt and how you hurt them.

*"Examine me, O God, and know my mind; test me, and discover . . .*
*if there is any evil in me and guide me in the everlasting way."*
*(Psalm 139:23 – 24, GNT)*

Please note: If you have been in an abusive relationship, especially as a small child, you can find great freedom in this part of the inventory. You see that you had **NO** part, **NO** responsibility for the cause of the resentment. By simply writing the words "none" or "not guilty" in column 5, you can begin to be free from the misplaced shame and guilt you have carried with you.

Celebrate Recovery has rewritten Step 4 for those who have been sexually or physically abused:

> Made a searching and fearless moral inventory of ourselves, realizing all wrongs can be forgiven. Renounce the lie that the abuse was our fault.

## More tools

1. Memorize Isaiah 1:18 (TLB): "Come, let's talk this over! says the Lord; no matter how deep the stain of your sins, I can take it out and make you as clean as freshly fallen snow. Even if you are stained as red as crimson, I can make you white as wool!"
2. Read the Principle 4 "Balancing the Scale" verses on page 29.
3. Keep your inventory balanced. List both the good and the bad! This is very important! As God reveals the good things that you have done in the past, or are doing in the present, list them on the reverse side of your copies of the "Celebrate Recovery Principle 4 Inventory Worksheet."
4. Continue to develop your support team.
5. Pray continuously.

# Principle 4 Verses

## Balancing the Scale

| **Emotion** | **Positive Scripture** |
|---|---|
| Helplessness | *"For God is at work within you, helping you to want to obey him, and then helping you do what he wants." (Philippians 2:13, TLB)* |
| Dwelling on the past | *"When someone becomes a Christian he becomes a brand new person inside. He is not the same any more. A new life has begun!" (2 Corinthians 5:17, TLB)* |
| Wanting | *"And it is he who will supply all your needs from his riches in glory, because of what Christ Jesus has done for us." (Philippians 4:19, TLB)* |
| Loneliness | *Jesus says, "I am with you always." (Matthew 28:20, TLB)* |
| Oppression, Trouble | *"All who are oppressed may come to him. He is a refuge for them in their times of trouble." (Psalm 9:9, TLB)* |
| Fear, Doubt | *"Yes, be bold and strong! Banish fear and doubt! For remember, the Lord your God is with you wherever you go." (Joshua 1:9, TLB)* |
| Melancholy, Apathy | *"This is the day the Lord has made. We will rejoice and be glad in it." (Psalm 118:24, TLB)* |
| Worry | *"Let him have all your worries and cares, for he is always thinking about you and watching everything that concerns you." (1 Peter 5:7, TLB)* |

# Celebrate Recovery
# Principle 4 Inventory Worksheet

| **1. The Person** | **2. The Cause** | **3. The Effect** |
|---|---|---|
| Who is the object of my resentment or fear? | What specific action did that person take that hurt me? | What effect did that action have on my life? |

*"Let us examine our ways and test them, and let us return to the LORD." (Lamentations 3:40)*

| **4. The Damage** | **5. My Part** |
|---|---|
| What damage did that action do to my basic social, security, and/or sexual instincts? | What part of the resentment am I responsible for?<br><br>Who are the people I have hurt?<br><br>How have I hurt them? |

Lesson 10

# Spiritual Inventory Part I

**Principle 4**: Openly examine and confess my faults to myself, to God, and to someone I trust.

*"Happy are the pure in heart." (Matthew 5:8)*

**Step 4**: We made a searching and fearless moral inventory of ourselves.

*"Let us examine our ways and test them, and let us return to the Lord." (Lamentations 3:40)*

## Think About It

*"Search me, O God, and know my heart: test my thoughts. Point out anything you find in me that makes you sad, and lead me along the path of everlasting life." (Psalm 139:23 – 24, TLB)*

The following list gives some of our additional shortcomings (sins) that can prevent God from working effectively in our lives. Reading through it and searching your heart will help you get started on your inventory!

## Relationship with others

*"Forgive us our sins, just as we have forgiven those who have sinned against us. Don't bring us into temptation, but deliver us from the Evil One." (Matthew 6:12 – 13, TLB)*

- Who has hurt you?
- Against whom have you been holding a grudge?
- Against whom are you seeking revenge?
- Are you jealous of someone else?

(Note: The people who you name in these areas will go in column 1 of your Celebrate Recovery Principle 4 Inventory Worksheet.)

- Who have you hurt?
- Who have you criticized or gossiped about?
- Have you justified your bad attitude by saying it is "their" fault?

(Note: The people who you name in these areas will go in column 5 of your Celebrate Recovery Principle 4 Inventory Worksheet.)

## Priorities in life

*"He will give them to you if you give him first place in your life and live as he wants you to." (Matthew 6:33, TLB)*

- After accepting Jesus Christ, in what areas of your life are you still not putting God first?
- What in your past is interfering with you doing God's will? Your ambition? Pleasures? Job? Hobbies? Money? Friendships? Personal goals?

## Attitude

*"Get rid of all bitterness, passion, and anger. No more shouting or insults, no more hateful feelings of any sort." (Ephesians 4:31, GNT)*

- Have you always complained about your circumstances?
- In what areas of your life are you ungrateful?
- Have you gotten angry and easily blown up at people?
- Have you been sarcastic?
- What in your past is causing you fear or anxiety?

## Integrity

*"Do not lie to each other. You have left your old sinful life and the things you did before." (Colossians 3:9, NCV)*

- In what past dealing were you dishonest?
- Have you stolen things?
- Have you exaggerated to make yourself look better?
- In what areas of your past have you used false humility?
- Have you lived one way in front of your Christian friends and another way at home or at work?

Have you memorized Isaiah 1:18 (TLB) yet?

*"Come, let's talk this over! says the Lord; no matter how deep the stain of your sins, I can take it out and make you as clean as freshly fallen snow. Even if you are stained as red as crimson, I can make you white as wool!"*

---

**Write About It**

1. Relationship with Others

    - Who has hurt you? (Go as far back as you can). How did they specifically hurt you?

- Who are you holding a grudge against? (Seeking revenge?)

- Who are you jealous of? (Past and present.) Why?

- Who have you hurt? And how did you hurt them?

- Who have you been critical of or gossiped about? Why?

- How have you attempted to place the blame on someone else? (Be specific).

- What new healthy relationships have you developed since you have been in recovery?

2. Priorities in Life

   - What areas of your life have you been able to turn over to your Higher Power, Jesus Christ?

   - After acting on Principle 3, in what areas of your life are you still not putting God first? Why not?

   - What in your past is keeping you from seeking and following God's will for your life?

- Number the following list in order of your personal priorities.

  ____ career
  ____ family
  ____ church
  ____ Christ
  ____ friendships
  ____ money
  ____ ministry

- What are your personal goals for the next ninety days? (Keep it simple!)

3. Attitude

   - What areas in your life are you thankful for?

   - In the past, what things have you been ungrateful over?

- What causes you to lose your temper?

- To whom have you been sarcastic to in the past? (Give examples).

- What in your past are you still worried about?

- How has your attitude improved since you have been in recovery?

4. Integrity

   - In the past, how have you exaggerated to make yourself look good? (Give examples.)

   - Does your walk as a Christian match your talk? Are your actions the same at recovery meetings, church, home, and work?

   - In what areas of your past have you used false humility to impress someone?

   - Have any of your past business dealings been dishonest? Have you ever stolen things?

- List the ways you have been able to get out of your denial (distorted /dishonest thinking) into God's truth.

# Spiritual Inventory Part 2

**Principle 4**: Openly examine and confess my faults to myself, to God, and to someone I trust.

*"Happy are the pure in heart." (Matthew 5:8)*

**Step 4**: We made a searching and fearless moral inventory of ourselves.

*"Let us examine our ways and test them, and let us return to the Lord." (Lamentations 3:40)*

## Think About It

*"Search me, O God, and know my heart: test my thoughts. Point out anything you find in me that makes you sad, and lead me along the path of everlasting life." (Psalm 139:23 – 24, TLB)*

The following list gives the second half of the list of our shortcomings (sins) that can prevent God from working effectively in our lives. Reading through it and searching your heart will help you get started on your inventory!

**Y**our mind

*"Do not conform to the pattern of this world, but be transformed by the renewing of your mind. Then you will be able to test and approve what God's will is — his good, pleasing and perfect will." (Romans 12:2)*

- How have you guarded your mind in the past? Denial?
- Have you filled your mind with hurtful and unhealthy movies, television programs, internet sites, magazines, or books?
- Have you failed to concentrate on the positive truths of the Bible?

**Y**our body

*"Haven't you yet learned that your body is the home of the Holy Spirit God gave you, and that he lives within you? Your own body does not belong to you. For God has bought you with a great price. So use every part of your body to give glory back to God, because he owns it." (1 Corinthians 6:19 – 20, TLB)*

- In what ways in the past have you mistreated your body?
- Have you abused alcohol and drugs? Food? Sex?
- What past activities or habits caused harm to your physical health?

**Y**our family

*"But if you are unwilling to obey the Lord, then decide today whom you will obey. . . . But as for me and my family, we will serve the Lord." (Joshua 24:15, TLB)*

- In the past, have your mistreated anyone in your family?
- Who in your family do you have a resentment against?
- Who do you owe an amends to?
- What is the family secret that you have been denying?

## Your church

*"Let us not neglect our church meetings, as some people do, but encourage and warn each other, especially now that the day of his coming back again is drawing near." (Hebrews 10:25, TLB)*

- Have you been faithful to your church in the past?
- Have you been critical rather than active?
- In the past have you discouraged your family's support of their church?

As you continue your inventory, commit Psalm 139:23 – 24 (TLB) to memory and use it as a prayer:

*Search me, O God, and know my heart; test my thoughts. Point out anything you find in me that makes you sad, and lead me along the path of everlasting life.*

**Write About It**

1. Your Mind

   - Since accepting Christ as your Higher Power, how has God transformed your mind (Romans 12:2)? What worldly standards have you given up?

- How have you used denial to attempt to guard your mind?

- Have you filled or are you filling your mind with hurtful and unhealthy movies, television programs, Internet sites, magazines, or books?

- How have you failed to concentrate on the positive truths of the Bible? (Be specific.)

2. Your Body

   - What past activities or habits caused harm to your physical health?

- In what ways have you mistreated your body?

- If you have abused alcohol, drugs, foods, or sex, how did they negatively affect your body?

- What have you done to restore God's temple?

3. Your Family

    - Have you mistreated anyone in your family verbally, emotionally, or physically?

- Who in your family do you hold a resentment against? Why?

- Can you think of anyone to whom you owe amends? Why? ( Don't worry about actually making them now! That's Principle 6.)

- What is the "family secret" that you have kept denying?

- How have relationships improved since you have been in recovery? (Be specific.)

4. Your Church

- How would you rate your past participation in your church?

  ____ Very involved
  ____ Semiactive member
  ____ Sideline member
  ____ Attender
  ____ Went only on holidays
  ____ Never attended

- Prior to your recovery, what was your main reason for going to church?

- Have you ever tried to discourage any family members from church involvement? How? Why?

- How has your commitment to your church increased since starting your recovery? (Give examples.)

# Afterword

When you complete all five lessons to the best of your ability, CONGRATULATIONS are most definitely in order! Now you are ready to move to the next part of Principle 4: confessing your faults to God, yourself, and another person you trust. Taking this step will move you into freedom from your past. Not only will you find freedom as you share the secrets of your past with another person, but you will also receive the "perfect freedom" of Christ's complete forgiveness for all your past shortcomings and sins. That's Good News!